HOW DOES A BIRD FLY?

Kate Woodward

Designed by Mary Forster
Illustrated by Isabel Bowring

Consultant: Robin Horner (Warden, RSPB)

CONTENTS

Additional illustrations by Joseph McEwan and Guy Smith

Early fliers

Some of the creatures that lived on Earth over 200 million years ago, at the same time as the dinosaurs, could fly. They were called pterosaurs.

pterosaur

Pterosaurs had wings made of leathery skin, not feathers. For this reason, scientists do not count them as birds.

Some pterosaurs had wings about 7m (almost 26ft) across. That's nearly as long as a bus.

Pterosaurs had jaws like beaks.

Compsognathus

None of the dinosaurs could fly.

The first bird

The first animal that scientists call a bird is the Archaeopteryx. It lived about 140 million years ago. They think it developed from dinosaurs that could not fly, not from pterosaurs.

It was about the size of a crow and had feathers on its body and wings.

Archaeopteryx

Odd bird

This Hoatzin chick is similar to the earliest known birds. It has unusual claws on its wings, like an Archaeopteryx (see below). It lives in the forests of South America today.

The claws drop off the adult bird.

Fossil bird

Scientists have found the remains, or fossils, of Archaeopteryxes buried inside rock.

It had teeth and had claws on its wings to climb trees.

All kinds of birds

There are more than 8,650 kinds of birds in the world today and they are all very different. They live in places as cold as the North Pole and as hot as the tropical rainforests around the Equator.

Ostriches live on the grasslands in Africa. They cannot fly, but can run very fast.

ostrich

budgie

Budgerigars are popular pets. Wild budgies live in large groups, or flocks, in Australia.

Geese live near water. Their young are called goslings.

goose and gosling

penguin

Some penguins live in the Antarctic near the South Pole. They are very good swimmers, but cannot fly.

A bird's body

To help birds to fly, their bodies are very light and streamlined. This means they are a smooth shape so they slip through the air easily. Here you can see the parts of a bird's body.

Feathers

Birds are the only animals with feathers. Small birds have about 1,000 feathers. Large birds can have as many as 25,000.

Eggs in a nest

All birds lay eggs. They do this so they do not have to carry their young around inside them before they are born.

Wings

Birds have wings instead of arms. They are strong and light enough to make a bird fly when it flaps them.

Feathers are made of keratin, like our hair.

Eyes

Many birds have eyes on opposite sides of their head so they can see as much around them as possible.

chick

This beak is good for catching fish.

Beak

Birds have different shaped beaks depending on what food they eat.

Neck

Birds have very bendy necks. They can turn their heads to point backwards to clean themselves with their beaks.

Ears

A bird's ears are hard to see. But they can hear very quiet sounds.

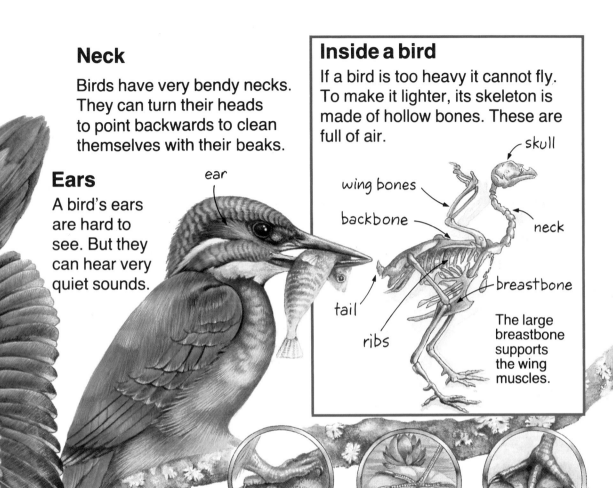

Inside a bird

If a bird is too heavy it cannot fly. To make it lighter, its skeleton is made of hollow bones. These are full of air.

skull

wing bones

backbone

neck

tail

breastbone

ribs

The large breastbone supports the wing muscles.

Feet

Birds' feet vary in shape and size. Many use their toes to grip branches.

A kingfisher's feet are covered in scaly skin.

A lily trotter has very long toes to walk over soft mud.

A goose has webbed feet which it uses for paddling.

5

Feathers

Feathers keep birds warm, stop their bodies from getting wet and help them to fly. All birds have different types of feathers. You can see them on this drake (male duck).

Down feathers

Down feathers are the very soft ones next to the bird's skin. They help keep the bird warm.

Tail feathers

Birds use their tail feathers to steer themselves in the air and to balance on the ground.

A woodpecker uses its tail to hold itself steady against a tree.

Wing feathers

The long feathers on the wings are the most important in helping the bird to fly.

The feathers on a bird's body are called its plumage.

wing feathers

tail feathers

mallard

body feathers

Body feathers

Body feathers lie smoothly over the down feathers. They are oily so that they are waterproof. This stops the bird getting cold and wet.

Moulting

Adult birds lose old feathers a few at a time and grow new ones. This is called moulting.

Cleaning and preening

Birds spend a lot of time looking after their feathers to keep them clean and healthy. They pull each feather through the tip of their beak. This is called preening.

scarlet macaw

Preening gets rid of tiny insects, such as lice, which like to live in feathers.

Feather colour

Some birds have bright feathers so they get noticed. This helps them attract a mate.   lorikeet

Others have feathers the same colour as the things around them, so they are hard to see and can hide from enemies.
grouse

A flamingo has pink feathers. This colour comes from the food it eats.   flamingo

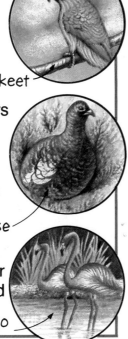

Taking a bath

You can often see small birds bathing in water or in dust.

A bird gets dirt and lice off its feathers by rubbing itself in dust.

Make your own birdbath

Small birds like to splash in water. You can make a birdbath in your garden using an upturned old dustbin lid filled with water.

Borrow a bird book from your library to help you recognise birds that come to use it.

Built to fly

Three types of animals can fly – birds, bats and insects. Birds are the best fliers because of the shape of their wings.

Not a bird

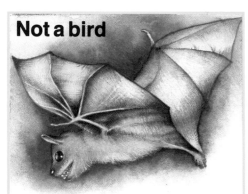

A bat is not a bird as it has no feathers. Its body is furry and it has leathery skin on its wings. It belongs to the type of animals called mammals.

Birdmen

In the past, men tried to fly like birds. They made wings and fixed them to their arms, but were too heavy to fly.

The wing

A bird's wing is a special shape, rounded on top and curved underneath. This is called an aerofoil and helps lift the bird as it flaps its wings.

In flight, air passes smoothly over the wing.

aerofoil shape

golden eagle

primary flight feathers

Primary means "first". The long primary feathers are the main ones that power the bird through the air.

secondary flight feathers

The secondary flight feathers help make the aerofoil shape.

wing coverts

The wing coverts help make the wing rounded on top.

In flight

A bird flaps its wings forward and down. The feathers are held flat to push against the air. The bird flies forwards.

The bird brings its wings upwards and back to start another flap. As it does, the feathers twist open to let air through.

To change direction or go up and down, the bird tilts its body to one side and moves its wings or tail to steer through the air.

Make your own aerofoil

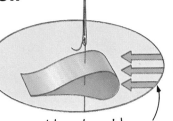

1

glue here

2

blow hard here

3

air on top presses less

air below pushes up

1. Bend a long piece of paper into an aerofoil shape. Glue the ends together and a little way up the side edges as shown.

2. Using a needle, thread cotton through the middle of the paper*. Blow hard over the curved end of the paper. What happens?

3. Air rushes fast over the top of the aerofoil. This air presses less against the aerofoil than air below, so the aerofoil rises up.

*Get an adult to help you.

Different ways to fly

The shape of a bird's wing tells you something about how it flies. Next to the birds on these pages is a small picture of their wing shapes to help you recognise them.

Speedy swallows

A swallow has curved, pointed wings. This good aerofoil shape makes the air rush fast over the top of them. Swallows flap their wings very fast to speed along.

It tucks its short legs into its body while it is flying so they do not slow it down.

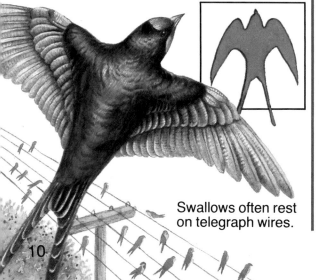

Swallows often rest on telegraph wires.

Fastest bird

The peregrine falcon is a bird of prey. This means that it hunts other small birds and animals.

When it hunts, it circles high in the sky looking for prey.

Once it has spotted something, it dives at about 180kph (112mph) with its wings back. This is almost as fast as a racing car. It is called stooping.

As it reaches its prey, the falcon swings its feet forwards and knocks the victim with its claws.

Long distance fliers

Many geese, such as these snow geese, fly very long distances to where they nest. They fly for many hours without stopping and have long, broad wings which they do not need to flap very fast.

Geese often make a 'honking' noise as they fly.

Straight from the nest

Once a chick is strong enough it flies straight from its nest. At first, it makes short, practice flights from bush to bush.

A mother tempts her chicks out of the nest with food.

Short flights

A jay has wide, blunt wings which it flaps slowly. This makes it easy to twist and turn through trees.

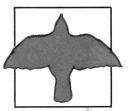

Birds with wings this shape usually only fly for short distances.

11

Flying with the wind

Many birds use the wind to help them stay up in the air. Some keep their wings still and let the wind carry them along. Others beat their wings against the air to stay in one spot.

Riding on air

Many large birds stay in the air for a long time without flapping their wings. This is called gliding.

An albatross has very long, narrow wings for fast gliding over the sea.

An albatross hardly flaps its wings at all. It can fly like this for days just using the wind.

It spends most of its life out at sea and is rarely seen, except by sailors.

Gliding over the sea

1

2

3

wind

1. The bird flies with the wind down towards the sea.

2. Flying fast, it turns towards the wind and rises up.

3. Then it turns and flies fast with the wind again.

High fliers

When the sun heats the ground, warm air spirals upwards. These draughts of warm air are called thermals. Most large birds of prey use their long wings to soar upwards on thermals.

Once it is at the top of a thermal it glides down to reach another.

thermal

The bird is carried up high by the rising warm air. It does not need to flap its wings.

Vultures can soar for many hours at a time without becoming exhausted.

Staying in one spot

Many birds beat their wings fast against the air to stay in one spot. This is called hovering. A hummingbird hovers to feed.

It beats its wings in a figure of eight shape nearly 50 times every second.

Bird spotting

Try to recognise everyday birds by their wing shape. Draw them, then check in a guide to see what type they are.

Going up and coming down

Birds may live in trees, on water or on cliff tops so they take-off and land in different ways. Most take off by springing into the air.

Running take-off

Large birds are too heavy to spring up. This coot has to run fast for a long way, splashing across the water, before it gets up in the air.

It stretches its neck out to make itself more streamlined.

Using sea breezes

Cormorants nest on cliff tops where there are strong sea breezes. They jump off cliffs with their wings open so the wind lifts them up.

Cormorants live in large groups called colonies.

Lazy flier

Pheasants do not like flying much. But if they are frightened they flap their broad wings and take off almost straight up in the air.

Their wings are short so they do not hit branches and trees.

Landing on a branch

All birds have to slow down before they can land safely.

As a bullfinch comes in to land it spreads its tail feathers out like a fan.

The feathers act like a brake and slow down the bird's flight.

It brings its feet forward ready to land.

It flaps its wings back and forwards to slow it down more.

Landing on water

A swan is one of the heaviest flying birds.

Swans land on water. They put their large webbed feet down first and push against the water. This slows them down before they land. They look as if they are water-skiing.

Its toes grip tight around the branch as it lands, so it does not fall off.

As it settles, the bird closes its tail feathers and tucks in its wings.

15

Migration

Many kinds of birds fly from one part of the world to another every year. This is called migration. They make this long journey to a warmer place where there is plenty of food.

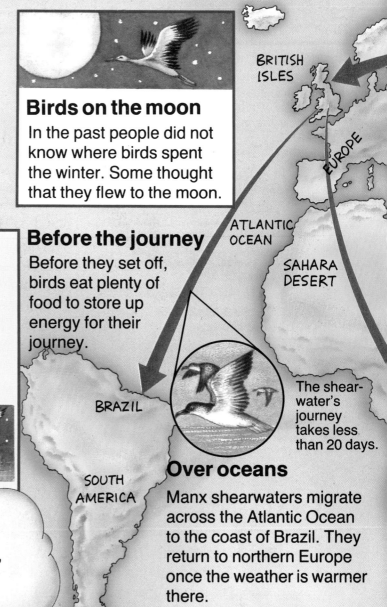

Birds on the moon

In the past people did not know where birds spent the winter. Some thought that they flew to the moon.

BRITISH ISLES

EUROPE

ATLANTIC OCEAN

SAHARA DESERT

Following stars

Birds find their way by watching the sun during the day and following the stars by night. Something inside them acts like a clock. It tells them when to set off.

Bad weather

During bad weather, when the sun is hidden by clouds, birds can lose their way.

Before the journey

Before they set off, birds eat plenty of food to store up energy for their journey.

BRAZIL

SOUTH AMERICA

The shear-water's journey takes less than 20 days.

Over oceans

Manx shearwaters migrate across the Atlantic Ocean to the coast of Brazil. They return to northern Europe once the weather is warmer there.

SIBERIA

One goose leads and
the others follow in a
"V" pattern.

Out of the Arctic

Whooper
swans nest in
Siberia in the Arctic Circle.
In winter many fly to north-
west Europe.

Over mountains

Bar-headed geese
cross the Himalaya
mountains at over
8,000m (26,000ft),
as high as some
jet planes cruise.

HIMALAYAS

INDIA

ARABIAN
SEA

AFRICA

The willow
warbler flies
non-stop for four
days and nights
to cross the
desert.

Studying birds

Sometimes migrating birds are
shot for sport. Ornithologists
(people who study birds)
count the birds
to see if there
are fewer of one
type. Then they
try and protect
them from
hunters.

Over deserts

The tiny willow warbler flies
more than 4,000km (2,400
miles) from Europe across
the Sahara Desert to Africa.

Be an ornithologist

Look out for migrating birds
gathering on telegraph wires
before they leave in autumn. Find
out which birds arrive in spring to
tell you warm weather is coming.

17

Night owls

Most owls do not fly about much during the day. This is because they are roosting, or sleeping. They come out at night to hunt.

Night hunters

Owls are good at hunting at night. Their wings, eyes and ears are specially made to make flying and hunting in the dark easier.

A tawny owl has shorter wings than some other owls, for flying among trees.

Owls have huge eyes. Some are almost as big as human eyes.

tawny owl

facial disc

Their ears are behind the face feathers, called the facial disc, at the side of their head.

Owls have sharp, hooked beaks for carrying and tearing up their food.

soft fringes

These sharp claws, called talons, are for catching and killing food.

An owl has soft fringes on the edge of its wing feathers. These help it fly almost silently, so that small animals do not hear it coming.

18

Protecting our owls

Some owls lose their homes and hunting grounds when farmers cut down trees to make new fields. You can find out which owls are threatened and how to help by joining a local bird club. Your library will help you find one.

Hunting for food

A barn owl is a very agile flier. It has large, broad wings which it flaps slowly. It can take-off vertically, stop suddenly in mid-flight and hover in one spot. It needs to do all these to hunt well.

barn owl

When he hears a mouse, he flies overhead and hovers for a moment. Then he pounces.

The owl glides silently through the air listening for sounds and watching the ground.

Waiting for supper

Before they can fly, the young owls wait at the nest for their parents to bring food.

At the last moment, he swings his sharp talons forward to catch the mouse.

19

Birds that cannot fly

There are a few birds that cannot fly. Some have found different ways to get around such as swimming or running, so they no longer need to fly.

Champion swimmers

Penguins cannot fly because their wings have become more like flippers. They use them to swim.

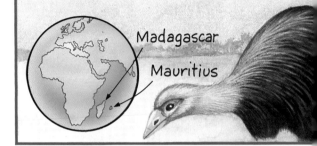

Birds of the past

The giant elephant bird once lived on Madagascar and the dodo on Mauritius, both islands off Africa.

Madagascar

Mauritius

Their flippers are short and thin, like paddles. They are good for pushing themselves along underwater.

Penguins have a very thick layer of tightly-packed feathers covering their bodies to help keep them warm in the frozen Antarctic.

emperor penguin

They swim near the surface of the water and dive down to catch fish.

When people went to live there, they hunted the birds and stole their eggs. Soon there were no birds left.

dodo

elephant bird

They could not fly to safety as they had such tiny wings.

Flightless cormorants

Cormorants living on the Galapagos Islands have no enemies. They have lost the ability to fly because they do not need to.

They have plenty of food to eat from the seas around the islands.

Adélie penguins often march one after the other, "following the leader", across the snow.

adélie penguin

They waddle as they walk, using their flippers to balance.

Too heavy to fly

An ostrich is about 2.5m (8ft) tall and weighs 150kg (330lbs), nearly as much as two adults. It is too heavy to fly, but runs very fast. Its ancestors could not fly.

Birds which weigh more than 15-20kg (30-45lbs) are too heavy to fly.

Amazing fliers

On this page you can find out about some amazing flying feats.

Non-stop flier

Swifts can fly for up to three years non-stop. They eat, drink, bathe and sleep as they fly.

One swift lived for 16 years and could have flown up to eight million km (nearly five million miles). This equals about 200 times around the world.

Biggest flying bird

The Andean condor is the biggest flying bird in the world. Its wings spread out from tip to tip are 3.2m (nearly 11ft). It uses them to glide in thermal currents.

Its wings are nearly four times the length of your arms outstretched.

The greatest traveller

The Arctic tern makes the longest migration of all birds. Each year it flies from the Arctic Circle to the Antarctic and back again, to spend the summer at each Pole in turn.

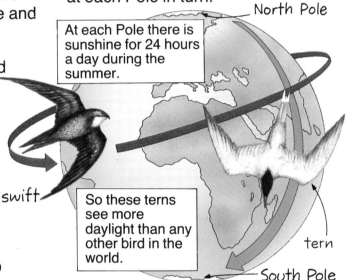

North Pole

At each Pole there is sunshine for 24 hours a day during the summer.

swift

So these terns see more daylight than any other bird in the world.

tern

South Pole

Smallest bird

The bee hummingbird from Cuba is the smallest bird in the world. It is only 57mm (2¼ inches) from beak to tail. This is about as long as your thumb.

The hummingbird gets its name from the noise its wings make as it hovers.

Rarest of all

Although there are lots of birds, some are becoming rare. Like the dodo they could die out unless we look after them and protect their homes.

Shot to extinction

There were once thousands of passenger pigeons in America.

None of these pigeons is alive today because they were all shot down and killed for sport.

Secret nests

Not long ago there were only a few ospreys living in Britain. Their nests had to be kept secret so no-one could steal their eggs.

Never steal eggs from a bird's nest.

Birds of the rain forest

Every day, large areas of rain forests are chopped down and burned. The birds who live there are in danger of dying out because they are losing their homes.

hyacinth macaw

toucan

hummingbird

Andean cock of the rock

rosella

Index

First published in 1991. Usborne Publishing Ltd, Usborne House, 83-85 Saffron Hill, London EC1N 8RT, England. Copyright © 1991 Usborne Publishing Ltd.